EDGE
BOOKS™

GROSS

GROSS RECIPES

GUIDES

by Kelsi Turner Tjernagel

CAPSTONE PRESS
a capstone imprint

Edge Books are published by Capstone Press,
1710 Roe Crest Drive, North Mankato, Minnesota 56003
www.capstonepub.com

Library of Congress Cataloging-in-Publication Data
Cataloging-in-publication information is on file with the Library of Congress.
ISBN 978-1-4296-9925-9 (library binding)
ISBN 978-1-4765-1406-2 (ebook pdf)

Editorial Credits
Mandy Robbins, editor; Tracy McCabe, designer; Marcie Spence, media researcher;
Sarah Schuette, photo stylist; Laura Manthe, production specialist

Photo Credits
Capstone Studio: Karon Dubke, cover, 4 (middle), 6, 7 (bottom), 8 (left), 9, 10 (right),
11, 12-13, 15, 16 (bottom), 19, 20 (left), 21, 22 (right), 22-23, 24 (right), 25, 26, 27, 28,
29 (left); iStockphoto: jam4travel, 10 (middle), John A. Meents, cover (food coloring);
Shutterstock: Alessio Cola, 8 (right), Crepesoles, (left), Eric Gevaert, 17 (bottom), Eric
Isselee, 18, Deklofenak, cover (chef), GorillaAttack, cover (ketchup), HamsterMan
20 (right), Igor Klimov, 7 (right), Joe Belanger, cover (egg), Luis Santos 29 (middle),
Madlen, cover (design element), Mikael Damkier, 14 (right), motorolka, 5, Nataliia
Natykach, 16 (top), Nattika, 29 (right), Nikola Tsvetkov, 14 (left), nito, cover (blender),
Pan Xunbin, 4 (top), 24 (left), Peredniakina, cover (design element), schankz,
24 (bottom), Steve Collender, 10 (top), SunnyS, cover (peanut butter), Svetlana
Kuznetsova, 17 (middle), Tsekhmister, 4 (bottom), Willyam Bradberry, cover
(design element)

Printed in the United States of America in Brainerd, Minnesota.
092012   006938BANGS13

Table of Contents

Getting Gross in the Kitchen

What are puke, eyeballs, worms, and blood doing in the kitchen? You'll find the answers within these pages. Whether you want to gross out your friends or satisfy your hunger, you'll find a recipe here. Choose a recipe, grab your tools, and prepare your ingredients. It's time to shock your taste buds and your friends and family.

Kitchen Safety

When it comes to gross recipes, fake blood is a blast. But we don't want any real blood taking away from the fun. Here are some tips to help you stay safe in the kitchen:

-Ask an adult to help. Whether you're boiling or baking, you'll want an adult nearby to help or to answer questions. And always get an adult's help when using sharp knives.

-Keep a first-aid kit nearby. Accidents happen, and it's always a good idea to be prepared. A basic first-aid kit contains bandages, a cream or spray to treat burns, alcohol wipes, and a small scissors.

-Wash Up. No one wants to eat the bacteria living on your hands and under your fingernails. Before starting any recipe, make sure to wash your hands.

-Cover Up. Always wear oven mitts or use pot holders to take hot pans out of the oven.

Gather up your supplies, and get ready for some seriously gross eats!

WIGGLY, WORMS

Host a worm-eating contest! Serve these wiggly creations to anyone bold enough to slurp one down. The cherry taste and slippery, smooth texture make these worms a bizarre delight.

Tools:

200 flexible straws, clean cardboard ½-gallon (2-liter) milk or juice carton, scissors, baking sheet, parchment paper, 1-gallon (4-l) size plastic bag, rolling pin, serving plate

Ingredients:

Great Value. Cherry Gelatin Dessert Naturally & artificially flavored NET WT 3 OZ (85g)

6 6-ounce (170-gram) packages cherry gelatin
4 cups (1 liter) boiling water
20 drops green food coloring
12 chocolate sandwich cookies

WAGGLY

1 Extend each straw to full length. Place them upside down in the carton.

2 With the help of an adult, mix the cherry gelatin powder and boiling water. Stir until gelatin is dissolved.

3 Add food coloring to the gelatin mixture and stir.

4 Pour the mixture over the straw openings. Then place the carton in the refrigerator to chill overnight.

5 To remove the straws from the carton, use the scissors to cut the long edge of the carton. Tear away the sides of the carton from the straws.

6 To remove the worms from the straws, run hot water over each straw for a few seconds. The top of each straw should have an empty space. Starting at the empty end, squeeze each worm out.

7 As you remove the worms, place them on a baking sheet covered with parchment paper. Store the sheet in the refrigerator until the worms can be served.

8 Place the chocolate cookies in the plastic bag. Crush the cookies with a rolling pin.

9 Spread the crushed cookies on a serving plate. Then place the worms on the "dirt."

7

Cleaning out the litter box never tasted so good. Are you gutsy enough to try a bite?

KITTY LITTER

Tools:
2 cake pans, 1-gallon (4-l) size freezer bag, rolling pin, small bowl, extra large mixing bowl, rubber scraper, mixing spoon, new kitty litter box, microwave-safe dish

Ingredients:

1 chocolate cake mix

1 white cake mix

ingredients to prepare cake mixes

2 sleeves graham crackers

1 teaspoon (5 milliliters) water

5 drops green food coloring

3 cups (720 mL) vanilla yogurt

½ cup (120 mL) shredded coconut

12 small chocolate chews (Tootsie Rolls work well)

1 Bake the cakes according to package instructions.

2 Place the graham crackers in the freezer bag. Crush the crackers with the rolling pin.

3 In a small bowl, combine the water and green food coloring. Add 1 cup (240 mL) graham cracker crumbs. Mix until the crumbs are green. Set aside.

4 Once cakes are cooled, crumble into a large bowl. Mix in yogurt, coconut, and half the plain cracker crumbs. Dump into a new, clean litter box.

5 Heat three chocolate chews in a microwave-safe dish for five seconds. Shape them to look like cat poop. Bury the "poop" in the cake mixture. Repeat with three more chocolate chews.

6 Spread the remaining plain cracker crumbs over the cake. Sprinkle the green cracker crumbs on top.

7 Heat the remaining six chocolate chews in the microwave three at a time. Shape them and place them on top of the crumbs.

CAKE

TIP: Heating only three chocolate chews at a time prevents them from cooling off before you can shape them.

BOGUS BLOOD

Unleash your inner vampire! Use this bloody concoction as a dip for some delicious cookies. You'll make a bloody mess and enjoy a mouth-watering snack.

Tools:

medium microwave-safe bowl, rubber scraper

Ingredients:

2 tablespoons (30 mL) cornstarch

½ cup (120 mL) corn syrup

¼ cup (60 mL) cold water

20 drops red food coloring

1 drop green food coloring

Ever wonder why blood is red? Hemoglobin is found in red blood cells. Hemoglobin contains a pigment that gives blood its red color.

1 In a microwave-safe bowl, combine the cornstarch and half of the corn syrup.

2 Add the remaining half of the corn syrup and stir.

3 Add the cold water. Stir.

4 Add the red and green food coloring. Stir.

5 Cover the bowl. Microwave the mixture for two minutes or until it just starts to boil.

6 Stir mixture, and let it cool.

TIP: Be careful where you put that blood—it stains. Keep it away from carpet, clothes, and anything you don't want permanently red.

concoction—something created by mixing several different things together

hemoglobin—a substance in red blood cells that carries oxygen and gives blood its red color

SNOT

Boogers never tasted so good!
Shock your friends and satisfy your
appetite with this slippery surprise.
The smooth gelatin and chunky tapioca
make a perfectly nasty-looking pair.
You can even add whipped cream on top!

Tools:

bowl,
rubber spatula,
hand mixer

Ingredients:

1 3-ounce (90-g) package lime gelatin
1 15.5-ounce (440-g) container tapioca pudding

1 In a bowl, prepare
the gelatin according
to package instructions.
Allow it to solidify.

2 Use the spatula to
scoop the tapioca into
the bowl with the gelatin.
Blend them together
using a hand mixer.

SURPRISE

TIP: While blending, keep the beaters of the hand mixer in the gelatin and tapioca mixture. Otherwise you'll end up taking a snot shower!

DO EAT THE

Double-dog dare your friends and family to eat this dog doo. These yummy treats look unappealing, but they taste amazing. Don't forget to provide doggie bags for the leftovers–if there are any!

Tools:

medium saucepan, mixing spoon, baking sheet, waxed paper

Ingredients:

½ cup (120 mL) milk

½ cup (120 mL) butter

1 cup (240 mL) white sugar

1 cup (240 mL) brown sugar

⅓ cup (120 mL) cocoa powder

1 cup (240 mL) chunky peanut butter

¼ cup (60 mL) chopped peanuts

¼ cup (60 mL) shredded coconut

3 cups (720 mL) rolled oats

1 teaspoon (5 mL) vanilla extract

DOG DOO

1 Add milk, butter, and sugars to a saucepan over medium heat.

2 Increase the heat to medium-high. With the help of an adult, stir the ingredients until the mixture comes to a gentle boil. Boil for one minute, while stirring constantly.

3 Remove the mixture from heat.

4 Add cocoa powder, peanut butter, peanuts, coconut, rolled oats, and vanilla extract. Stir until the mixture is the same **consistency**.

5 Let the mixture cool for 10 minutes.

6 Roll clumps of the mixture into mounds that look like dog poop. Cool the "poop" on a baking sheet covered with waxed paper.

➡ **consistency—how thick or thin something is**

GREEN SLIME SMOOTHIE

Your friends won't believe their taste buds when they drink this green slime! Thanks to the fruit and honey, this nutritious drink is also a sweet treat. After one swig, this may be your new favorite treat.

Tools:

paring knife, cutting board, blender, drinking glass

Ingredients:

1 apple
2 bananas
1 orange
2 stalks kale
2 cups (480 mL) water

1 cup (240 mL) fresh spinach
1 tablespoon (15 mL) honey

1 Rinse all of your produce with tap water.

2 Ask an adult to help you slice an apple into quarters on a cutting board. Cut out the apple's core and chop the apple into small pieces.

3 Peel the bananas. Cut them into bite-size pieces.

4 Peel the orange. Break it into sections.

5 Remove the kale stems. To do this, grab the stem of the kale in one hand. Then slide the leafy part through your other hand.

6 Put all of the ingredients in the blender. Place the lid securely on the blender, and blend until smooth.

7 Pour into a drinking glass and serve.

COW PIES

Don't live on a farm? It doesn't matter. These cow pies are the perfect solution for an after-school snack wherever you live. Combining chocolate and peanut butter makes this a winning recipe, even if it looks like cow dung.

Ingredients:

1 cup (240 mL) chocolate chips
½ cup (120 mL) chunky peanut butter
1 ½ cups (360 mL) rolled oats

1 Place the chocolate chips in a microwave-safe bowl. Heat them in the microwave for one minute. Remove the chips from the microwave, and stir until smooth.

2 Add peanut butter to the melted chocolate. Heat mixture for 30 seconds. Stir until smooth.

3 Add the rolled oats. Stir until the mixture is **uniform**.

4 Pour the mixture onto a baking sheet covered with waxed paper. Pouring from directly above makes the pies mound up in the center and ooze out on the edges like real cow dung.

5 Place the tray in the refrigerator or freezer to cool.

uniform—having the same appearance and thickness throughout

BITTER BARF

The best part of this recipe may just be the sound effects that you create. Don't forget to hold your stomach! It looks more believable. Unlike the other recipes in this book, this one is **NOT** delicious. You could eat it, but you probably wouldn't want to.

Tools:

2 medium bowls, rubber scraper

Ingredients:

½ cup (120 mL) rolled oats

½ cup (120 mL) crushed cereal of your choice

1 teaspoon (5 mL) cocoa powder

1 cup (240 mL) cottage cheese

½ cup (120 mL) applesauce

1 mashed banana

¾ cup (175 mL) vinegar

1 In a medium bowl, combine rolled oats, cereal, and cocoa powder.

2 In another bowl, combine cottage cheese, applesauce, banana, and vinegar.

3 Add the dry ingredients to the wet ingredients. Stir until the mixture is uniform.

CRISPY, COCKROACHES

Real cockroaches are disgusting. But these cockroaches are delicious and nutritious. Time to get crunching!

Tools:

small bowl, mixing spoon, cutting board, paring knife

Ingredients:

¼ cup (60 mL) plain Greek yogurt
¼ cup (60 mL) cream cheese
¼ cup (60 mL) chopped pecans
12 pitted dates
1 scallion

pitted—when the pit is removed from a fruit

CRUNCHY

1 In a small bowl, stir yogurt, cream cheese, and pecans until uniform.

2 With the help of an adult, slice an opening along the length of the dates.

3 Fill each date with the yogurt and cream cheese mixture.

4 Slice the green part of the scallion into 1-inch (2.5-cm) sections. Cut these sections lengthwise into small slivers. Stick two slivers into each "cockroach" to look like antennae.

FACT

People around the world have always eaten insects. Grasshoppers, termites, and other insects are still considered lunch in some countries.

WORM SANDWICHES

Regular hot dogs are boring.
Add some excitement to your plate
with a serving of these wild worms.
Don't worry-they're delicious!

Tools:

paring knife,
cutting board,
medium saucepan,
colander, mixing
spoon, large bowl

Ingredients:

1 package hot dogs
water
½ cup (120 mL) ketchup
1 tablespoon (15 mL) mustard
1 package hamburger buns

1 With the help of an adult, slice each hot dog lengthwise into four equal strips.

2 Put the sliced hot dogs in the saucepan. Add enough water to cover the hot dogs.

3 Boil hot dog strips for three minutes in the saucepan.

4 Turn off the heat, and let the water cool for five minutes.

5 Drain hot dog strips in a colander. Shake the colander to remove excess water.

6 Combine the ketchup and mustard in a large bowl. Add the hot dog strips and toss to coat.

7 Pile the worms high on hamburger buns, and enjoy!

colander—a kitchen utensil with holes, used for draining liquid off foods

EYE-POPPING PUPILS

Don't roll your eyes!
These eyeballs are part
of a balanced diet.

Tools:

colander,
towel,
spoon

Ingredients:

1 20-ounce (570 g) can of lychees

1 6-ounce (170-g) container
raspberry yogurt

½ cup (120 mL) dried cranberries

A lychee is the fruit of a tree that is native to China. The fruit's brittle outer covering is pink. The flesh of the lychee fruit is white. It tastes sweet and mild. Canned lychees are found in many grocery stores. Many specialty food shops also keep them on hand.

1 Drain the lychees in a colander. Pat them dry with a clean towel.

2 Fill each lychee opening with raspberry yogurt.

3 Place a dried cranberry into the yogurt.

lychee—the oval fruit of a tree from the soapberry family

FUNKY

These funky fingers get two thumbs up!
Not only do they look real, but they are
finger-licking delicious. Offer to make
hot dogs for dinner for your family.
Then surprise them with these!

FINGERS

Tools:
paring knife,
cutting board,
medium saucepan,
colander, towel,
serving dish

Ingredients:

4 hot dogs
4 large pieces of yellow onion
1 tablespoon (15 mL) mayonnaise
3 tablespoons (45 mL) barbecue sauce

1 With an adult's help, cut 1 inch (2.5 cm) off one end of each hot dog.

2 Halfway up each hot dog, make three shallow slices across the hot dog. These slices will be the "knuckles."

3 Boil hot dogs for three minutes in the saucepan.

4 Turn off heat, and let the water cool for five minutes.

5 Drain the hot dogs in a colander. Pat them dry with a clean towel.

6 Ask an adult to help you cut a small, flat space at the tip of the hot dog to make a nail bed.

7 Have the adult help you cut three pieces of yellow onion into slices that look like fingernails.

8 Using a dab of mayonnaise as glue, press an onion "nail" onto each "fingertip."

9 Fill a serving dish with barbecue sauce. Bury the bottom ends of your "fingers" in the sauce.

Glossary

colander (KOL-uhn-dur)—a kitchen utensil with holes, used for draining liquid off foods

concoction (kon-KOK-shuhn)—something created by mixing several different things together

consistency (kuhn-SIS-tuhn-see)—how thick, thin, or firm something is

hemoglobin (HEE-muh-gloh-bin)—a substance in red blood cells that carries oxygen and gives blood its red color

lychee (LEE-chee)—the oval fruit of a tree from the soapberry family

pitted (PIT-uhd)—when the pit is removed from a fruit

pupil (PYOO-puhl)—the round, dark center of your eye that lets in light

uniform (YOO-nuh-form)—having the same appearance and thickness throughout

Read More

Larrew, Brekka Hervey. *Wormy Apple Croissants and Other Halloween Recipes.* Fun Food for Cool Cooks Mankato, Minn.: Capstone Press, 2008.

Thomas, Lyn. *100% Pure Fake: Gross Out Your Friends and Family with 25 Great Special Effects!* Tonawanda, N.Y.: Kids Can Press, 2009.

Williams, Zac. *Little Monsters Cookbook: Recipes and Photographs.* Layton, Utah: Gibbs Smith, 2010.

Internet Sites

FactHound offers a safe, fun way to find Internet sites related to this book. All of the sites on FactHound have been researched by our staff.

Here's all you do:

Visit *www.facthound.com*

Type in this code: 9781429699259

 Check out projects, games and lots more at **www.capstonekids.com**

Index